D0486816

AS
Revise
PE
for
Edexcel

AS UNIT I

Participation in Sport and Recreation

by

Dennis Roscoe
Bob Davis
Jan Roscoe

AS Revise PE for Edexcel

by

Dennis Roscoe
Bob Davis
Jan Roscoe

BLACKBURN COLLEGE
LIBRARY
Acc No. BB29005
Class No. 796 RoS
Date Feb 2010

Jan Roscoe Publications

Text copyright to Dennis Roscoe, Jan Roscoe, Bob Davis.

Graphics copyright to Jan Roscoe Publications, Bob Davis.

All rights reserved. No part of this publication may be reproduced, or transmitted in any form or by any means, electronic or mechanical, including photocopy, recording or any information storage and retrieval system, without permission in writing from the publisher.

Published as 978-1-901424-54-6 in 2009 by Jan Roscoe Publications.

'Holyrood'
23 Stockswell Road
Widnes
Cheshire
WA8 4PJ
United Kingdom

tel: 0151 420 4446
fax: 0151 495 2622
e-mail: sales@jroscoe.co.uk

A Catalogue record for this book is available from the British Library

ISBN   Published as 978-1-901424-54-6

Cover designs by Helen Roscoe.

Published via Adobe InDesign, CorelDraw 10.410, Adobe Illustrator 9.0, Smartdraw 6.0

Laid out and typeset by

Macpro Design
e-mail: john@macprodesign.co.uk

Printed and bound by

Poplar Services
Poplar House
Jackson Street
St Helens
WA9 3AP

tel: 01744 23363
fax: 01744 451242

www.poplarservices.com

INTRODUCTION

Examination courses in Physical Education and Sport Studies have now become established within the post-16 curriculum and are a very popular and successful part of school, college or higher education.

This new edition has been written to address the change in content and style of the Edexcel AS Physical Education syllabus which commenced in September 2008.

This Physical Education course is multidisciplinary in nature, covering anatomy and physiology and contemporary studies including a small amount of comparative studies and historical studies. These subject areas have generated a substantial quantity of specialist literature each with its own specific language. At times you may be overwhelmed by the amount of material covered in such a one year examination course. 'AS Revise PE for Edexcel' addresses the problem of dealing with copious notes by summarising the content of the subject matter and attempting to explain in simple language what are sometimes complicated concepts or issues. Practice questions are provided at the end of each syllabus section, with answers at the end of the book. The answers will amplify the subject matter and provide clues as to how the exam itself should be approached. A new feature this time is the requirement that the final exam questions on each section of the syllabus shall include an essay type answer. This allows students to express their ability and knowledge in the context of properly written language (prose) with attention to grammar and punctuation.

Materials are presented in a concise and visual approach for effective and efficient revision. Modern terminology, nomenclature and units have been used wherever possible. At the end of the book there is a comprehensive index available for easy reference.

HOW TO USE THIS REVISION GUIDE

The ideal use of this Revision Guide would be to purchase it at the start of the course and relate each of the summary pages to the specific areas of the syllabus as an aide memoire. The inclusion of specific questions and full answers provide a means of self-testing. Don't be tempted to find out the answers before attempting a question.

In reality, whole examination questions contain a much broader content than those given in this guide. Examiners will attempt to examine more than one small area of the syllabus within the context of one full question and therefore it is important that you revise all aspects of your syllabus.

The main use of the Revision Guide should be during the final revision period leading up to your examinations, as it should help you to understand and apply concepts i.e. link summary content with examination question.

The aim of this Student Guide is to provide an aid that enhances syllabus analysis, and to raise your level of success in examinations.

THE QUALITY OF AUTHORS

We are an expert team of writers, who have considerable experience in teaching 'A' Level Physical Education, who have written past and current examination syllabuses, who have set and marked examination questions within this subject area and taught at revision workshops throughout the UK. Much of the material within this book has been thoroughly student tested.

We hope that this Revision Guide will prove useful to staff and students. Jan Roscoe Publications will welcome any comments you would wish to make about the book's utility or layout. Thank you for using our work.

Dennis Roscoe
Jan Roscoe

ACKNOWLEDGMENTS

We would like to thank Bob Davis for his co-operation and adherence to our demanding deadlines, and John Norris of Macprodesign for his patience in setting out the book and creating equanimity among the graphics and text. We thank Pete Rich for his painstaking proofing of the text. We thank Poplar Services for their patience in linking our work to their computers, and JRP staff member Linda Underwood for working hard in the background while I put this book together. We thank Helen Roscoe for her contribution as cover designer and photographer and Lois Cresswell for her patience as photographic model. We thank members of the Belgian Olympic Athletics Squad for permission to use their images. Lynn Goodkin has also been patient enough to proof read the text.

Dennis Roscoe
Editor

ACKNOWLEDGMENTS FOR GRAPHICS

Figure 1.1	istockphoto johnny scriv
Figure 1.7	istockphoto Ed Hidden
Figure 1.8	istockphoto Simone van den Berg
Figure 1.9	istockphoto Ron Summers
Figure 1.15	istockphoto Tammy Peluso
Figure 3.19	istockphoto Damir Spanic
Figure 3.20	istockphoto nikada
Figure 5.6	istockphoto Christopher O'Driscoll
Figure 5.7	istockphoto Soubrette
Figure 6.3	istockphoto Birgitte Magnus
Figure 6.11	istockphoto Sue McDonald
Figure 6.11	istockphoto Trevor Nielson
Figure 6.14	istockphoto Ludovic Rhodes
Figure 9.8	courtesy of Anwar El Bizanto
Figure 9.10	istockphoto webphotographeer
Figure 10.2	istockphoto Sophia Tsibikaki
Figure 10.3	istockphoto Grafissimo
Figure 10.6	istockphoto purdue 9394
Figure 11.1	Sport in the GDR magazine 1970
Figure 11.2	Sport in the GDR magazine 1972
Figure 12.1	istockphoto Mike Dabell
Figure 12.2	istockphoto Tim Kiusalaas
Figure 13.9	istockphoto Ben Blankenburg
Figure 13.13	istockphoto Joe Gough

All other photographs / graphics are by Helen Roscoe, Jan Roscoe, Dennis Roscoe or Bob Davis.

NEW for September 2009

JRP

HIGH QUALITY PHOTOS

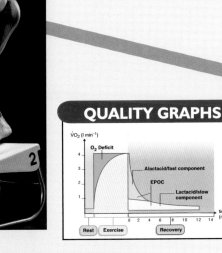

**ROSCOE et al
A2 Revise PE for Edexcel**
ISBN 978-1-901424-55-3

**A2
Revise
PE
for
Edexcel**

Dennis Roscoe
Bob Davis
Jan Roscoe

Jan Roscoe Publications

JRP

QUALITY GRAPHS

$\dot{V}O_2$ (l min⁻¹)

O_2 Deficit

Alactacid/fast component

EPOC

Lactacid/slow component

time (minutes)

Rest | Exercise | Recovery

REVISION SUMMARY NOTES

S.M.A.R.T.E.R. goals

SPECIFIC
    directly related a sporting situation.
MEASURABLE
    progress can be assessed.
ACCEPTED
    by both performer and coach.
REALISTIC
    challenging but within the capability of performer.
TIME PHASED
    a date is set for completion.
EXCITING
    inspiring and rewarding to the performer.
RECORDED
    written down.

REVISION SUMMARY CHARTS

active | passive
static | **STATIC STRETCHING** | PNF
dynamic | **DYNAMIC STRETCHING** | ballistic

This new Revise Series covers all aspects of the examinable A2 Edexcel syllabus commencing September 2009. The book consists of student notes, full colour illustrations, photographs, exam questions and full answers. Key concepts are clearly defined with examples that can be used in answers to exam questions, thus enabling the student to self-text. This student revision guide supports a comprehensive revision plan and will enhance student grades.

PRACTICE QUESTIONS & ANSWERS

6) How has modern technical developments influenced performance in sport today?   **5 marks**
Answer
- *Equipment such as the javelin allows it to be thrown farther.*
- *All-weather surfaces allow games to be played when grass would not and improves performance.*
- *Athletic tracks are faster today producing higher standards.*
- *The timing of races is now more accurate improving confidence.*
- *Better media communications have stimulated interest.*
- *In car racing, modern cars are faster, but safer.*
- *Specialised footwear for athletics and climbing.*
- *Research into swimming and water resistance.*
- *TV evidence used in cricket and rugby.*
- *Fitness suites for improving strength and mobility.*

HOW TO ORDER

tel +44(0)151 420 4446
(open every day 9am-5pm)

fax +44(0)151 495 2622
(open 24 hours a day)

email sales@jroscoe.co.uk

by post to: **JRP Publications, 'Holyrood', 23 Stockswell Road, Widnes, Cheshire WA8 4PJ, United Kingdom**

For **full listings** see the **JRP Catalogue** or visit **www.jroscoe.co.uk**

Jan Roscoe Publications
Sport and PE curriculum resources

- Buy all your books from us
- Purchasing Helpline
- Competitive Discounts
- Product Database
- Exhibitions on Request
- Book Jacket Service
- Price Promotions
- Website Ordering
- Online Catalogue
- Next Day Delivery
- Exclusive Offers
- Visit our Warehouse

CATALOGUE 2009

AS Revise PE for Edexcel

AS UNIT 1: Participation in Sport and Recreation

SECTION 1.1

HEALTHY AND ACTIVE LIFESTYLES

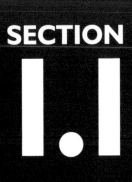
HEALTHY & ACTIVES LIFESTYLES

CHAPTER 1: The development of active leisure and recreation

Requirements for participation

Fitness, ability, resources and time

It is necessary to understand a series of **concepts**, **categories** and **benefits** associated with participation in **active leisure**. It is also necessary to look at the **cause** of problems and hence we need to be aware of the effects of **inactivity**.

Fitness

Fitness can be explained as the condition of the body and mind at any one time. Health, age, free time and more general lifestyle features must always be taken into account when assessing a desirable level of fitness.

Fitness means different things to different people. Comparing a 50 year old housewife with a top athlete, you can see that to be fit enough to cope with daily tasks would not be enough for the athlete.

Health-related **fitness** can be described as '**a basic level of physical fitness components which facilitate a good level of health**'.

See page 22 below for a full definition of fitness, and page 72 onwards for a discussion of physical fitness components.

Ability

The **ability** of an individual will vary according to health, age and free time. **Ability** is the foundation of the learning process, and to be successful a performer must have certain abilities which are **genetically determined**. This means that we are born with our abilities, they are **innate**. This contrasts with skills which are learnt by practice or observation of others with varying degrees of success. Abilities are also **enduring**, which means that people usually continue to display their ability for a long time.

Actual **ability** will need to be assessed against the potential ability and social constraints such as **opportunity**, **provision** and **self-esteem**.

Resources

Provision of **resources** for active leisure and sport for all age groups will remain an issue for the UK. Despite massive improvements in recreational provision, 'Sport for All' remains a policy which cannot be fully enacted at the moment.

Time

Time is the most critical feature of modern life, particularly the availability and positive use of **free time**. As our society has become more affluent and social discrimination has been reduced, there are increasing concerns about obesity and related diseases, sedentary lifestyles, and stress in an ageing population. We hope to develop a healthy society pursuing lifelong active leisure by considering these factors.

figure 1.1 – children's activities as active leisure

Concepts of recreation and active leisure

Physical activity appears to be a necessary experience for the development of a balanced, active and **healthy lifestyle**. It is explained as **gross motor movement**, in which parts of the body are highly active and moved vigorously.

Leisure

Leisure can incorporate a number of different activities, many of which do not involve physical activity (see figure 1.2).

Definitions of **leisure** include:

'**An activity, apart from the obligations of work, family and society, to which the individual turns of his / her own free will.**'

Crucial features of leisure are:

- It has a **social** function.
- It requires **free time**.
- It is more than an **activity**, also an **experience**.
- It is **self-realising**.
- It is **socialising** and **civilising**.
- It is undertaken as **free choice**.
- It can improve **health** and fitness.

figure 1.2 – leisure

Recreation

Recreation (figure 1.3) is a **positive** aspect of **leisure** and is widely described as **active leisure**. Its **characteristics** are similar to leisure in that it carries the individual and group away from the usual serious concerns of life. The attitudes derived from recreation involve healthy **contentment** and **relaxation** from mental anxiety.

The common **definition** of recreation is '**a pleasurable occupation of leisure time**'.

figure 1.3 – recreation

Recreational sport and 'Sport for All'

This section briefly explains what **sport** is, so that we can describe how the UK attempts to provide '**Sport for All**'.

Sports and pastimes are commonly used terms which describe a variety of sporting activities. They are as old as civilisation and contain many features and values originally developed in ancient times. See page 100 onwards in section 1.2 for a discussion in detail on this topic.

Regular, modern, **institutionalised sport**, on the other hand, was a 19th century European development of **athleticism** and **Modern Olympism**. The development of sport is also discussed below on page 103 onwards. Figure 1.4 shows how we break down the categories of sport into modern groupings.

Sporting activities take the form of a **struggle** with oneself or involve **competition** with others. Sport is **institutionalised**, not only in the context of being regular and organised, but regulated by a code of behaviour.

Fitness is a feature of sport and physical exercise, and we explain this concept further on page 22 below, as different **components** of fitness are relevant to different sports or activities.

There are two levels at which sport can operate, as a **recreational** activity and as an experience involving **excellence**. The discussion in chapter 10 page 121 below explains how the sports development pyramid links the two levels – depending on a sports performer's skill level, ability and motivation, and the opportunities provided.

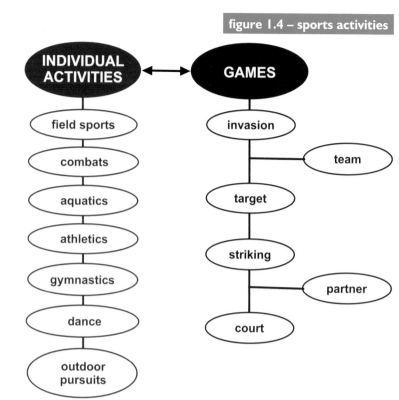

figure 1.4 – sports activities

Mass participation and 'Sport for All'

From 1972, the UK government established a policy in which the slogan '**Sport for All**' was used to attempt **mass participation** in sport as a spring-board to promote healthy lifestyles. This also acts as the base of the pyramid for elite sport or sporting excellence. The idea of a sports development pyramid explains the notion **that mass participation** involves many people trying out activities in order that a few may progress to excellence or elite sport.

There are three strands to the current 'Sport for All' policy, looking at **children and youth**, **adults**, and the **elderly**. See figure 1.5 for an outline of the factors affecting opportunity and provision for these groups. The figure also looks at a wider view of sport and participation. It is this breadth of participation including activities across a full spectrum (see figure 1.5) which may make it possible to achieve 'Sport for All'.

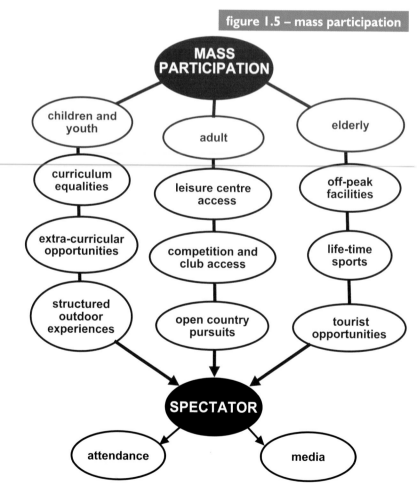

figure 1.5 – mass participation

Contemporary concerns

Obesity

Obesity is a major problem in our affluent society linked with poor eating habits and lack of sufficient physical activity. Statistics show that obesity is widespread in all age groups, but there is a particular concern over young children and older people. The risks for children lie with poor health in the future. The risks for older people are the facts of poor health now, with great danger of coronary heart disease (**CHD**) and poor mobility and the consequent lack of independence. Such factors for older people cause great expense to the nation, with the costs of health care and nursing support being very high.

Medical conditions linked with **obesity** and **inactivity** include coronary heart disease, diabetes, high blood pressure, high cholesterol and metabolic syndrome.

Obesity (figure 1.7) is defined as '**a surplus of adipose tissue resulting from excessive energy intake relative to energy expenditure**'.

The definition of obesity implies that the actual amount of body fat or its percentage of total weight can be estimated. The problem is that exact standards for allowable fat percentages have not been established. However, men with more than 25% body fat and women with more than 35% should be considered obese.

Positive energy balance

This definition of obesity highlights the major cause of obesity, namely an obese person would have energy intake far greater than energy output, which would be the result of inactivity and too much dietary fat intake.

This relationship is expressed as:

ENERGY INTAKE > ENERGY OUTPUT

to create a **positive energy balance**, which means that more energy is eaten (figure 1.8) as food than energy is used via exercise.

Excess carbohydrate (CHO) from food is stored as glycogen. When glycogen stores are filled, CHO together with excess fat intake are converted to fatty acids and glycerol, and then are stored as triglycerides or **fat** in adipose tissue. This is situated around major organs such as the heart and stomach, underneath the skin, and in skeletal muscle. Upper body obesity poses the most significant risk to disease.

Excessive weight gain is associated with certain health conditions such as **coronary heart disease** and **hypertension** (high blood pressure) with an increased risk of mortality and morbidity.

Controlling obesity

The only method of controlling obesity is to shift the energy relationship so that energy output exceeds energy intake – known as a **negative energy balance** and expressed as:

ENERGY INTAKE < ENERGY OUTPUT

This means that more energy is used via exercise than is eaten as food.

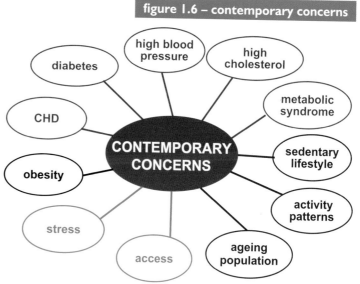

figure 1.6 – contemporary concerns

- diabetes
- high blood pressure
- high cholesterol
- CHD
- metabolic syndrome
- **CONTEMPORARY CONCERNS**
- obesity
- sedentary lifestyle
- activity patterns
- stress
- access
- ageing population

figure 1.7 – obesity and inactivity

figure 1.8 – less food required?

What is a good level of fat?

An **essential** (minimum requirement which would allow full body functions) body fat percentage for men is between 2% and 3% and for women between 8% and 12%. Normally **only** healthy elite athletes attain these percentages.

How is a person's body fatness related to good health?

Relative body fat is a major concern of athletes. Achieving a desired weight goal can lead to clinical eating disorders such as anorexia nervosa, which has occurred in some female endurance-based athletes. The restriction of food intake to levels well below energy expenditure causes anorexia nervosa.

The facts about obesity

The following facts about obesity should be noted:

- Over 30,000 deaths a year are caused by obesity – in England.
- 22% of the British adult population are obese.
- 75% of the British adult population are overweight.
- Child obesity has increased 3-fold in the last 20 years.

Coronary heart disease

As mentioned above, obese people have high risk factors of developing **coronary heart disease** (CHD). **CHD** is one of Britain's greatest killers and encompasses diseases such as **angina** and **heart attacks** or **coronary thrombosis**. Angina begins as a chest pain, which is due to ischemia. Ischemia is a condition in which there is a reduction in flow of blood and hence oxygen to the heart muscle itself. The first symptoms of **CHD** are usually noticed during physical exertion or excitement and the subsequent increase in heart rate. Heavy, cramp-like pains are experienced across the chest. Angina is normally treated and controlled with drugs and relaxation, but a person suffering from this condition has a higher risk of suffering from a **coronary thrombosis**.

Health risks from CHD can be reduced by regular aerobic exercise. This helps to maintain good coronary circulation (blood flow in the heart muscle itself), and strengthens and improves cardiac function, for example, resting heart rate is lowered.

Diabetes

Diabetes is a condition which occurs when a person's body cannot regulate glucose levels. Glucose is regulated by the release of the hormone insulin from the Isles of Langerhans situated in the pancreas. Too much glucose present in the bloodstream causes more insulin to be released to help remove it. If not enough glucose is present, the insulin available is reduced, and glucose levels are allowed to build up. The insulin enables the **transfer of glucose** from the blood into cells where it is needed for metabolism.

There are two types of diabetes:

- **Type 1 diabetes** usually occurs in younger people and is caused by the failure through disease of the mechanism for the production of insulin. This form of diabetes usually requires daily insulin injections for the rest of a person's life.
- **Type 2 diabetes** usually occurs in older people and is caused by age-related changes in the way the body reacts to insulin production.

Obesity is a major risk factor for type 2 diabetes.

Symptoms of type 2 diabetes are:

- Lack of circulation to the hands and feet.
- Extremes of thirst or hunger.
- Unexplained weight loss.
- Partial or total sight loss.

Regular aerobic exercise improves the regulation of blood glucose levels in the blood of type 2 diabetes sufferers. See page 24 below.

High blood pressure

Hypertension (high blood pressure) is a condition that occurs when a person's blood pressure is continually high, equal to or greater than 140/90 mmHg. High blood pressure is another condition associated with **obesity** and also with hardening of the arteries (arteriosclerosis). Arteriosclerosis is an age-related condition whose effects can be lessened by exercise continuing into old-age. Hypertension is a major contributing factor in atherosclerosis, coronary heart disease (CHD), and strokes.

High cholesterol

Cholesterol is a substance produced from fatty foods, particularly from a diet high in the saturated fats found exclusively in animal products. It is transported in the blood and to body tissues in the form of lipoproteins.

Two of the **lipoproteins** seem to have a relationship with the onset of coronary heart disease and have different amounts of cholesterol in their molecular make-up:

- **Low-density lipoprotein cholesterol** (LDL-C) contains high amounts of cholesterol and is known as '**bad cholesterol**'. If the digestive process does not remove this, it can lodge in the walls of arteries in the form of plaques causing the arteries to be narrower. This is a form of **atherosclerosis**.
  - Ideal level for blood LDL-C is less than 85 mg per decilitre of blood (mg/dl).
  - Risk level for blood LDL-C starts at above 110 mg/dl.
  - So the higher the level of LDL-C, the greater the risk of heart disease.

- **High-density lipoprotein cholesterol** (HDL-C) contains a high concentration of protein that is known as '**good cholesterol**'. It is thought that the HDL-C molecule helps prevent the process of atherosclerosis by blocking the movement of LDL-C into the arterial wall and by aiding the transport of cholesterol to the liver for removal by the body.
  - Ideal level for blood HDL-C is 70+ mg/dl.
  - Risk level for blood HDL-C starts at below 45 mg/dl.

Therefore, individuals with a high level of HDL-C seem to experience less coronary heart disease when compared to people who have high levels of LDL-C.

Exercise increases HDL-C and decreases LDL-C. Hence regular exercise helps keep arteries open and blood pressure (BP) lower than it otherwise would be. Blood pressure therefore tends to be more stable thus reducing hypertension.

The risk factors for high cholesterol are:
- Lack of exercise and / or **obesity**.
- Heredity.
- Age.

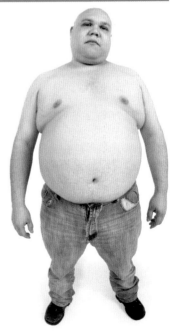

figure 1.9 – abdominal obesity

Metabolic syndrome

Metabolic syndrome is a term used to link coronary artery disease, hypertension, abnormal blood lipids (fats), **type 2 diabetes** and abdominal **obesity** to **insulin resistance**. The syndrome refers to the fact that some people develop a resistance of their muscle cells to the action of insulin, and therefore not enough glucose finds its way into the cells to enable them to work properly.

Hence cells (particularly muscle cells) will not have enough glucose to function properly - and the person feels **exhausted**.

The risk factors for this syndrome are:
- Arterial plaque build-up.
- **Excessive fat deposits** in the abdominal region (figure 1.9).
- High blood triglycerides, low HDL cholesterol and high LDL cholesterol.
- Raised blood pressure.

Roughly 20% of the population in the USA have this condition which makes type 2 diabetes worse, with the consequent risk of eyesight and circulation problems in older people.

Regular aerobic exercise reduces the risk of metabolic syndrome.

Sedentary lifestyles

The **sedentary** nature of modern life fails to give us the physical activity our bodies need for a long and active life.

Sedentary men and women are approximately twice as likely to suffer a fatal heart attack compared to their physically active friends.

Overall death rates from cancers, such as colon and breast cancer, are significantly higher among the sedentary population.

The **causes** of sedentary behaviour among adults and physical inactivity among children are:

- The increased availability of **transport**, for example, the car run to school in the mornings.
- Absence of the need to **walk** or **run**.
- The discouragement of vigorous play activities in the playground for children.
- The widening availability of **non-exercise** based recreational activities such as computer games.
- Limited physical education on the curriculum or extra-curriculum for children, with school fields being sold off or under-utilised.
- The actual increase in **leisure time**, which can mean less time spent being physically active at work or in physical recreations.
- The increase in white-collar (sedentary office based) working environments as opposed to the predominance of physically demanding blue-collar occupations of former times.

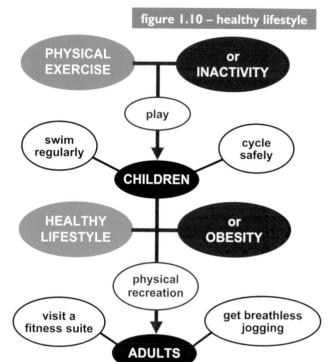

figure 1.10 – healthy lifestyle

Avoidance of the sedentary lifestyle

To achieve the **benefits** of physical exercise and to work towards a level of **fitness** in the interests of a healthy lifestyle (figure 1.10), the recommendations are:

- **Regularity** of exercise.
- A degree of exercise **intensity** sufficient to increase the heart rate over a period.
- The intention of **sustaining** this improved condition, thus promoting **long-term health**.
- Giving the individual a more **balanced attitude** towards **personal fitness**.
- For example, a minimum of exercise three times per week of 20 minutes duration and raising the pulse and breathing rates to 70% of maximum.

figure 1.11 – hypokinetic disorders

Hypokinetic disorders

Hypokinetic disorders (figure 1.11) are diseases or conditions that develop partly due to **insufficient exercise** directly linked to modern sedentary lifestyles. These include all the cardio-vascular diseases mentioned above, plus:

- **Osteoporosis**, which is an **age-related** condition in which **reduction of bone mass** takes place. This causes bone breakage and distortion, see page 24 below for the details.
- **Poor flexibility** as muscles, tendons and ligaments become shorter and tighter often resulting in **back pain** and other joint pain particularly in the knees and wrists.

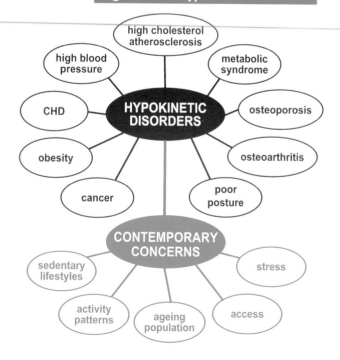

- Poor **posture** can eventually cause arthritic conditions of the back such as kyphosis (hunchback curvature of the upper spine), scoliosis or lordosis. Some of these conditions can be caused by inappropriate footwear (high heels?).
- **Osteoarthritis**, which is a condition where **joints** thicken with fluid-filled pockets, restricting joint flexibility.
- Some **cancers** (see above).

The importance of regular exercise in reducing the risk of hypokinetic disorders is discussed below in chapter 2 page 33.

Activity patterns

Activity patterns have also changed for **adults** caught up in taking in more calories than they use up. This is partly because eating out has become fashionable, and **fast food** and processed food is readily available. **Sedentary** jobs, **spectatorism** and **car use** have replaced physical work, active leisure, regular exercise and fresh food. Even though there is **more free time**, the use of that free time does not appear to compensate for a labour-saving and over-indulgent lifestyle.

Issues affecting health, the quality of life and age of death of an individual are:
- Diet and nutrition.
- Lack of physical activity.
- Smoking.
- Alcohol.
- Recreational drugs.

Ageing population

figure 1.12 – exercise while ageing

The gradually changing pattern in which lifestyle changes seem to be leading to poorer health is sometimes put down to an **ageing population**. Elderly people have perhaps not made the best use of leisure provision, but people are living longer. **Longevity** is an issue where people are living longer as improved nutrition, health care, and exercise regimes are having an effect on life chances. This means that there are far more people aged over 80 than ever before, and there are many 'retirement' towns where school rolls are decreasing. It means that fun runs and recreational classes for the elderly must be encouraged. The question of **access** has always been a particular problem for the elderly, where **mobility** is an issue. The regulations on access have been largely solved by legislation particularly for the disabled. But issues of access in terms of **availability** of facilities have not as yet been met, particularly in country areas.

Various conditions are caused by cellular deterioration with age. This deterioration can be slowed by exercise programmes for all ages:

- **Arteriosclerosis** is a hardening of the arteries usually occurring in older people, a process enhanced by lack of exercise. This happens mostly in the lower limbs, and involves a gradual calcification of the tunica media (causing muscle atrophy and hardening of this muscular middle wall of arteries), which does not allow blood to circulate at levels needed for exercise. This reduces older people's capacity for exercise.
- **Osteoporosis**, as mentioned above, is also called brittle bone disease, and is a major cause of bone breakage in older people.
- **Osteoarthritis** is a joint condition which can be very restrictive for older people.

As the average age of the population increases, there is a consequent increased risk of the above age-related conditions occurring. It is therefore even more important for all older people to exercise regularly (figure 1.12). This issue is discussed in greater detail on page 22 onwards.

Access in terms of opportunity and provision

The **opportunity** for various groups of people to participate in sport may be affected by the following cultural factors:
- Gender.
- Ethnicity / religion.
- Age.
- Disability.
- Social / economic class.

Provision is concerned with the facilities available to a potential performer and depends on the following issues:

- Inner city or countryside?
- Poor or rich neighbourhood?
- Regional hub nearby – and can the performer use it?
- Travel distance?
- Expensive equipment / kit required?

Stress

The phenomenon of **stress**-induced health issues has yet to be fully understood, but the pressure of work and life generally makes stress a major physical and mental problem. Active recreation should help to remove this stress and not only assist individuals, but reduce the time lost by employers.

Stress is a response of the body to any demands made on it. The symptoms of stress (figure 1.13) are **physiological**, **psychological** or **behavioural** (see table 1.1 below for details).

Stressors

Stressors (summarised in figure 1.14 below) are:

- **Social** including the disapproval of parents / peers, the rejection by peers / parents, or isolation from normal social interactions.
- **Chemical** or **biochemical** in which harm is inflicted by ingestion of nasty substances.
- **Bacterial**, which would be an illness caused by micro-organisms.
- **Physical** in which a person would suffer injury, pain or exhaustion.
- **Climatic** in which extremes of weather are experienced, such as hot weather for endurance activities, or rain and cold on bare skin.
- **Psychological**, in which there is a mismatch between the perception of the demands of a task and the ability of a person to cope with these demands.

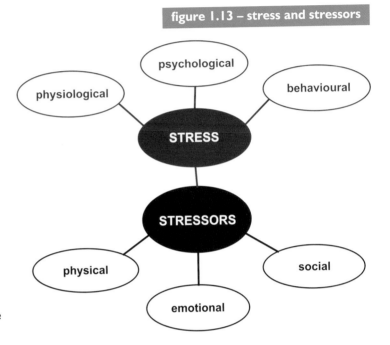

figure 1.13 – stress and stressors

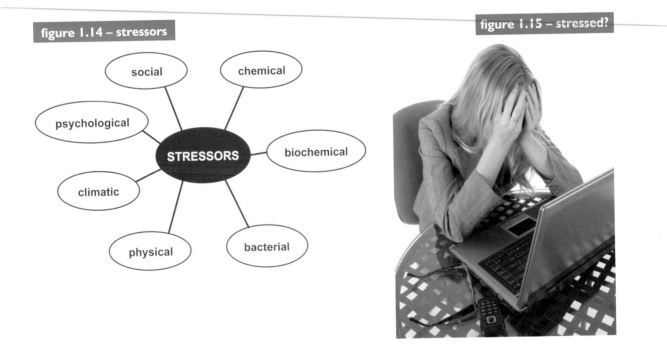

figure 1.14 – stressors

figure 1.15 – stressed?

Symptoms of stress

Table 1.1 – **symptoms of stress**

physiological symptoms	psychological symptoms	behavioural symptoms
increased heart rate	worry	rapid talking
increased blood pressure	feeling overwhelmed	nail biting
increased sweating	inability to make decisions	pacing
increased breathing rate	inability to concentrate	scowling
decreased flow of blood to the skin	inability to direct attention appropriately	yawning
increased oxygen uptake	narrowing of attention	trembling
dry mouth	feeling out of control	raised voice pitch
		frequent urination

Practice questions

1) Briefly outline **three** basic requirements an individual needs in order to participate in sport and recreation.   *3 marks*

2) Define and link the concepts of leisure and recreation.   *3 marks*

3) In relation to sport and recreation, what do the terms opportunity and provision mean? Illustrate your answer with an example.   *4 marks*

4) Identify possible physical objectives of a major game, swimming or athletics as part of your school / college sport programme.   *3 marks*

5) Describe **four** different ways in which a physical activity programme might be used to reduce obesity in children, choosing a different activity in each of your examples.   *4 marks*

6) What is the risk of death from coronary heart disease with a sedentary lifestyle as compared with an active lifestyle? Give **two** reasons to support your answer.   *3 marks*

7) The key to living a long and healthy life is to reduce the risk factors that lead to life-threatening diseases, often referred to as hypokinetic disorders.
   What is a hypokinetic disorder? Illustrate your answer with **two** examples of hypokinetic disorders and explain how regular aerobic exercise might reduce the risk factors associated with these hypokinetic disorders.   *5 marks*

8) What is cholesterol? What are the differences between and the effects of low-density lipoprotein cholesterol (LDL-C) and high-density lipoprotein cholesterol (HDL-C) on the human body?   *5 marks*

9) a) Explain **two** psychological symptoms of stress.   *2 marks*
   b) Identify **three** stressors in the context of sport.   *3 marks*

CHAPTER 2: Healthy lifestyle

Health, fitness and exercise

Exercise can be described as **physical exertion** of the body, done to achieve a good level of health and fitness - both mentally and physically. Exercise can vary from light, for example a steady walk, to intense, for example vigorous cycling or running.

A **healthy lifestyle** involves:

- Eating a healthy, **balanced diet**.
- Maintaining a healthy **body mass**.
- Getting the right amount of **exercise**.
- Minimising **stress**.
- Effectively combining work and **socialising**.

Definitions of health and fitness

Health is defined as '**a state of complete physical, social and mental well-being, free from mental and physical disease**'.

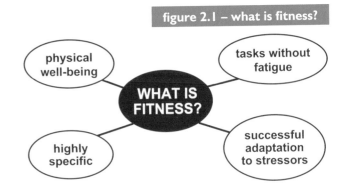

figure 2.1 – what is fitness?

A good **physical** state results from regular exercise, proper diet and nutrition, and proper rest for physical recovery. An athlete may be physically fit but emotionally unstable and therefore unhealthy.

Fitness can mean different things to different people (figure 2.1) and has been defined as '**the ability to carry out our daily tasks without undue fatigue**', or '**the successful adaptation to the stressors of one's lifestyle**' Dick (1989).

- When we examine these definitions we need to ask ourselves 'what does the person need to be fit for?' Dick's definition suggests that fitness is how well our bodies cope with and adapt to the stressors of daily life.
- Both definitions universally define fitness for all ages, gender and lifestyles. For example, fitness for an old age pensioner could be measured by his / her ability to walk the dog on a daily basis. In the case of global superstar Paula Radcliffe, fitness may be measured by her physical state of fitness to win her next marathon race.
- Fitness is also **highly specific** when you consider the anaerobic fitness requirements for a 100m sprint and the aerobic fitness requirements for long distance running.
- From this starting point we are able to build up a picture of the fitness requirements of an individual in relation to his / her required performance.

Positive health benefits of exercise

Figure 2.2 summarises the effects of exercise on health. The discussion below explains this.

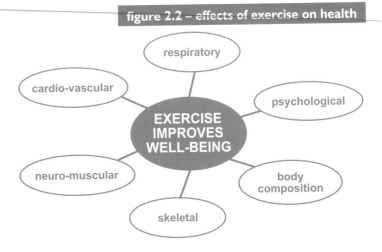

figure 2.2 – effects of exercise on health

Cardio-vascular

- Exercise slows down degenerative diseases such as coronary heart disease (CHD).
- Exercise increases high density lipoproteins (HDL-C) and decreases low density lipoproteins (LDL-C) (which is responsible for depositing cholesterol and narrowing the lumen of arteries), hence blood pressure remains stable thus preventing hypertension.

Respiratory

- Exercise slows down decline in $\dot{V}O_{2max}$ and hence aerobic capacity remains higher than it otherwise would be.
- Therefore the capability for long duration low intensity work remains higher.

Body composition

- Exercise reduces obesity by burning off excess fat during and after activity when the body's metabolic rate remains elevated.
- Cardiac workload (hence risk of CHD) is less with a lower body mass.
- The capability to move around (walk, run and climb) is therefore better with a lower body mass.
- Exercise relieves symptoms of osteoarthritis.

Skeletal

- Exercise stimulates the thickening and improved elasticity of cartilage.
- Exercise reduces the risk of osteoporosis by increasing bone density due to increased deposition of calcium (see page 24 below for details about osteoporosis).

Neuro-muscular

- Exercise sustains strength and co-ordination levels.
- Exercise enhances tensile strength and flexibility of tendons and ligaments thus allowing for a fuller range of joint movement.

figure 2.3 – aerobics as fun for health

Psychological

- Immediately following activity a person experiences a feeling of well-being and a reduction in anxiety.
- There will be a long-term increase in work performance and hence a more positive attitude to work.
- Improved self-esteem and self-efficacy.
- Benefits of social interaction.

Hopefully informed individuals will be able to make decisions about lifestyle choices that ultimately will improve their quality of health and fitness (see figure 2.3).

Physical benefits from exercise and being fit

Energy metabolism

Energy provides the means for any activity including movement using muscles attached to limbs, chemical activity in cells of the body, transmitting nerve signals, activity of the major organs of the body and so on.
Energy metabolism is the term used to describe **total intake of food** sufficient to supply enough **energy** to:

- Keep cells alive.
- Keep systems working.
- Meet the demands of life.

Basal metabolic rate (BMR)

The BMR is the **least rate of energy usage** needed to carry out **basic body functions**, and would be measured while lying down after 8 hours sleep or 12 hours fasting.

Typical values for men and women at 20 years of age are:
BMR_{male} = 100 kJ kg^{-1} per day   **BMR_{female} = 90 kJ kg^{-1} per day**
BMR_{male} = 0.069 kJ kg^{-1} min^{-1}   **BMR_{female} = 0.063 kJ kg^{-1} min^{-1}**

Total metabolic rate

Total metabolic rate is the sum of basal metabolic rate (**BMR**) + **energy required for all** daily activities. The total average energy usage for 18 year olds in the USA is 8,000 kJ per day for females, and 12,000 kJ per day for males. Table 2.1 below shows how different types of exercise contribute to metabolic rate.

Table 2.1 – **metabolic rate contribution by different activities**

activity	energy expenditure (kJ kg⁻¹ min⁻¹) over BMR
sitting at rest	0.10
walking	0.26
jogging and swimming (moderate)	0.6
cycling (moderate)	0.46
vigorous exercise	1.09

There is another factor which needs to be taken into consideration when calculating metabolic rate. This is the **SDA** (**specific dynamic action**) which is the extra rate of energy expenditure due to digestion, absorption of nutrients, and transport of nutrients to body cells. **SDA** is usually estimated as **10% of energy value of food** consumed.
It is therefore possible to calculate **total metabolic rate** (TMR) using the formula:

TMR = all energy expenditure due to exercise + BMR + SDA

Using body mass and time taken to perform the various exercise options listed above, it is possible to estimate total energy output of an individual.

Exercise, metabolic rate and obesity

Exercise increases the metabolic rate, thereby using up energy at a greater rate than normal and using the body's stored resources (fat). Metabolic rate remains elevated for some time after exercise. This means that energy from adipose tissue and energy from recently eaten food will continue to be used up at a rate which depends on how intense the exercise was. The facts about obesity have been outlined on page 15 above, and the fact of exercise using up stored energy will obviously affect the state of obesity in a person.

A negative energy balance: **ENERGY INTAKE < ENERGY OUTPUT** is the only sure way to combat obesity.

Osteoporosis

Osteoporosis has been outlined above as an age-related condition made worse by physical **inactivity**. In this condition **reduction of bone mass** takes place. This is due to **reabsorption of minerals** that form part of bone structure. The process of reabsorption makes **bones** porous, brittle and liable to break. Osteoporosis is linked with **hormonal** changes in post-menopausal females, but is also due to the lack of exercise which largely characterises this age group.

Research has shown that if bones are **mechanically** loaded (by applying forces to the bones along their length), then they tend to respond by becoming **stronger** with greater bone cell wall **thickness** and better **calcification** of bone tissue. This is the response that enables bones to heal when broken, a relatively rapid process in young people of both sexes. Exercise consisting of **weight bearing activities** will therefore reduce the risk of this condition, for example, walking, jogging, weight training and aerobics.

Type 2 diabetes management

As mentioned above on page 16, type 2 diabetes is an age-related condition in which there is an **imbalance of blood sugar** required for daily activities caused by **insulin resistance**. This is linked to obesity, coronary artery disease, stroke and hypertension.

However, if **exercise** is continued through middle-age and old-age (from page 40 onwards), **blood glucose** is broken down and hence the proportion of glucose carried by blood is reduced and the chances of type 2 diabetes reduced.

Muscle cell walls in people with type 2 diabetes become less permeable to glucose needed for exercise. Therefore normal levels of insulin can't transfer blood glucose into the cells for metabolism. This is known as **insulin resistance**.

But during exercise, **muscle contraction** increases cell membrane **permeability to glucose** which means glucose can pass naturally into the cells. This in turn means that cell requirement for insulin is reduced (called **insulin sensitivity**). This means that **acute bouts of exercise** reduce the effects of type 2 diabetes (note that this is **acute exercise!**).

Nutrition and weight management

A **balanced diet** is (figures 2.4 and 2.5) the combination and proportions of carbohydrates (CHO), fats, proteins, roughage, water and essential minerals and vitamins which best provide for a sportsperson's nutritional requirements. Table 2.2 gives the details of each food type and its contribution to life.

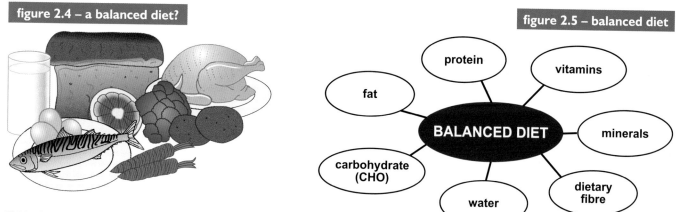

figure 2.4 – a balanced diet?

figure 2.5 – balanced diet

Table 2.2 – **summary of dietary content**

type of food / sources	function as a food fuel - how it is used	energy content (kJ g⁻¹)	percentage in a balanced diet
carbohydrate (CHO) sugars, rice, potatoes, pasta	**Main energy supply**. Absorbed as glucose in small intestine. Transported around body as blood glucose. Available for immediate energy. Excess stored as muscle and liver glycogen and as fat.	17	60 %
fats butter, oil, pastry, fried food	**Secondary energy supply**. Absorbed as fatty acids and glycerol in the small intestine. Stored as triglycerides in adipose tissue. Triglycerides conveyed to the liver via the circulatory system. In the liver they are converted to glucose. Available as delayed (20 minutes delay) energy source for long duration low intensity aerobic exercise.	39	20-25 %
proteins meat, eggs, milk, cheese, nuts	Absorbed as amino acids in the small intestine. Used for growth and repair by all tissues. Used as an energy source when the body is depleted of CHO and fat. Excess protein not needed for tissue repair is broken down and used as an energy supply.		10-15 %
vitamins	Organic substances needed for crucial functions in almost all bodily functions. Regulate metabolism and facilitate energy release. Have important functions in bone formation and tissue synthesis.		small amounts essential
minerals	Calcium provides structure in bones and teeth. Iron is needed for red blood cell production. Other minerals also assist in synthesising glycogen, fat and protein.		small amounts essential
dietary fibre wholegrain cereals, vegetables	Non-starch, structural polysaccharide including cellulose. Only available from plant sources. Gives bulk to food residues in the intestines. Aids gastrointestinal functioning.		large amounts necessary, 20 to 40 grams per day
water	Constitutes 72% of muscle weight and around 50% of adipose tissue. Provides the body's transport and reactive medium. Transports nutrients and leaves the body in urine and faeces. Lubricates joints, keeping bony surfaces from grinding against each other. Provides structure and form to the body. Some sports drinks are designed to meet both energy and fluid needs of athletes.		large amounts necessary, up to 5 litres per day

The need for a balanced diet

The food pyramid shown in figure 2.6 illustrates the approximate proportions of the different food groups which should be consumed in a balanced diet.

The foods in the lower part of the pyramid should form the main part of a balanced diet, while those at the top should be eaten in smaller quantities.

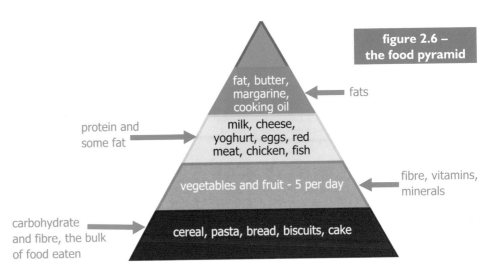

figure 2.6 – the food pyramid

fat, butter, margarine, cooking oil — fats

protein and some fat → milk, cheese, yoghurt, eggs, red meat, chicken, fish

fibre, vitamins, minerals → vegetables and fruit - 5 per day

carbohydrate and fibre, the bulk of food eaten → cereal, pasta, bread, biscuits, cake

Energy balance

When energy input is equal to energy output a **neutral energy balance** is achieved, as a result of which a person's weight remains constant. This concept can be expressed as:

ENERGY INPUT = ENERGY OUTPUT

This means that there would be no tendency for this person to add adipose tissue to his / her body structure.

Dietary requirements for exercise

Table 2.3 – **a comparison of daily energy intake for athletes**

activity	daily energy intake kJ – females	daily energy intake kJ – males
Tour de France		25000
triathlon		20000
rowing	12600	14700
swimming	8400	15500
hockey	9200	13400
soccer		14700
running	9200	13000
gymnastics	6000	
body building	5900	14500

STUDENT NOTE

Table 2.3 shows the variation in energy expended during competition and training (measured in kJ per day) in elite male and female endurance (figure 2.7), strength and team sport athletes. Except for high-energy intake of athletes at extremes of performance and training, the daily energy intake does not exceed 17000 kJ for men and 12500 kJ for women. Note that the difference between males and females can be accounted for by size difference. Values per kg of body mass would be similar.

Within rather broad bands, a balanced diet from a regular food intake provides the nutrient requirements for active individuals (as observed in the Food Pyramid figure 2.6). However, dietary requirements depend on the **intensity** and **duration** of the exercise period. This means developing a diet that is tailor-made to suit the needs of the individual.

Carbohydrate requirements

Glycogen is the most important and most valuable food for any type of exercise. Physically active individuals should obtain between 60% and 70% of daily energy intake from carbohydrates – particularly unrefined, low glycemic foods such as fresh acidic fruits (apples, pears, oranges) and most vegetables. The longer the duration of the activity, the greater the % of CHO intake.

figure 2.7 – endurance cyclists consume huge amounts of energy

In activity lasting longer than 90 minutes, as in the case of marathon running, dietary manipulation techniques, such as **carbo-loading**, will increase muscle glycogen stores to above normal levels. Carbo-loading is a process where extra carbohydrate is taken in after a short period of carbohydrate starvation.

For rapid carbohydrate **replenishment** after exercise, carbohydrate foods with a high glycemic index are recommended, for example, foods such as bananas, brown rice, pasta, raisins or wholemeal bread. Food should be eaten within two hours of completing the physical activity. This is because eating these foods will be more efficient in increasing blood glucose concentrations and hence stimulating the greater insulin release needed to convert glucose to glycogen.
Optimal glycogen replenishment will benefit individuals involved in regular intense physical activity, such as playing in tournaments that span over a period of days.

Protein requirements

Physically active individuals need more protein than inactive people do (between 1.2-1.4 grams per kg body mass per day). Additional protein intake is needed to compensate for increased muscle breakdown that occurs during and after intense exercise. Protein is also needed to build new muscle cells (known as muscle hypertrophy).

In strength and power-based activities, additional protein intake is recommended (between 1.4-1.8 grams per kg body mass per day).

Fat requirements

Fat intake should be restricted, unless additional body mass is required, as is the case for extreme performers such as sumo wrestlers.
Unsaturated fats are preferable to saturated fats.

Vitamin and mineral requirements

Getting the right balance of vitamins and minerals can be sourced from the daily-recommended intake of fresh fruit and vegetables.

When and what should you eat before an exercise period?

- Food should be eaten between 3-4 hours prior to the competition so that it is well digested and absorbed into the bloodstream.
- The meal needs to be high in carbohydrates, low in fat and moderate in fibre to aid the digestive process.
- An example meal could be pasta bake with spinach, a banana and a still flavoured drink.

Hydration

Exercise is thirsty work. Fluid loss during exercise depends on the intensity and duration of the exercise, temperature and humidity, body size and fitness levels. The longer and more intense the exercise period, for example in a long distance race, the more the need to drink before, during and after the event.

Bearing in mind that water comprises 60% of total body mass, it is important that **water balance** is maintained during exercise. **At rest**, water loss occurs via evaporation from the skin (sweat) and excretion with the majority lost as urine. Water intake will depend on climate and body mass. The modern fashion of carrying water bottles for ready consumption reflects modern concerns about water balance.

During exercise

During exercise, more water is produced during tissue respiration along with heat energy as a by-product of the metabolic process. In order to prevent the body from heating up too much, water is transported to the skin where sweating occurs. The loss of water from the skin by evaporation causes the skin to fall in temperature, and hence reduces the effect of heat production in muscle. But far more water is lost as sweat than is produced by tissue respiration, the amount of sweat being determined by external temperature, body mass and metabolic rate. There is increased water loss via expired air due to increased breathing, but the kidneys decrease urine flow in an attempt to decrease dehydration. The total effect is that the body loses more water than is produced or retained, and this must be replaced if exercise is to continue at a maximal rate.

In extreme exercise situations (for example during a marathon) 6-10% of body water content is lost, hence the need for water intake during exercise. This means that during 1 hour's exercise an average person could expect to lose around 1 litre of fluid, and even more in hot conditions. This could represent as much as 2 litres an hour in warm or humid conditions.

Dehydration and loss of performance

Excessive loss of fluid impairs performance as blood plasma volume decreases and body temperature rises. This process places extra strain on the heart, lungs and circulatory system, which means that the heart has to work harder to pump blood around the body.

Cholesterol

Cholesterol (see page 17 above for the details) is a substance produced from fatty foods particularly from a diet high in saturated fat. If this is not removed by the digestive process it can be deposited in arteries (causing them to be narrower), which is a form of atherosclerosis. During exercise you get an increase in high density lipoproteins (HDL-C) and decrease in low density lipoproteins (LDL-C, which are responsible for depositing cholesterol and narrowing the lumina of arteries). Hence exercise reduces atherosclerosis, and blood pressure (BP) becomes stable thus preventing hypertension.

Current trends in health

The following tables give a comparison between different countries as to various health-related concerns.

Table 2.4 – **general government expenditure on health as percentage of total government expenditure**

location	2000	2005
Mexico	11.4	12.5
United States of America	19.5	21.8
Egypt	7.5	7.3
Finland	10.2	11.6
Greece	10.1	11.5
Turkey	9.8	13.9
United Kingdom	14.8	16.2
China	1.1	1
Japan	15.7	17.8
New Zealand	16.2	18

STUDENT NOTE

In this list, the USA has the highest percentage of GDP expenditure on health – probably reflecting high expenditure on an increasingly ageing population.

What can be concluded from China's expenditure on health, and Turkey's increase in spend between 2000 and 2005?

Table 2.5 – **adult mortality rate (number of people dying between 15 and 60 years per 1000 population), both sexes**

location	2000	2006
Mexico	136	122
United States of America	114	109
Egypt	200	186
Finland	104	96
Greece	82	76
Turkey	152	123
United Kingdom	88	80
China	135	116
Japan	73	67
New Zealand	86	75

STUDENT NOTE

In this list, note that Egypt, Turkey and Mexico have the highest mortality rates. Japan, New Zealand and Greece have the lowest mortality rates.

Does this reflect way of life or concern about basic hygiene?

Table 2.6 – **life expectancy at birth (years), both sexes**

location	2000	2006
Mexico	73	74
United States of America	77	78
Egypt	66	68
Finland	78	79
Greece	78	80
Turkey	70	73
United Kingdom	78	79
China	71	73
Japan	81	83
New Zealand	79	80

STUDENT NOTE

In this list, the Japanese live the longest, just ahead of New Zealand and Greece. Egypt, China and Turkey have the lowest life expectancy among this group.

Could this be linked to health care provision, or more general lifestyle issues?

Table 2.7 – **deaths due to tuberculosis (per 100 000 population)**

location	2000	2006
Mexico	4	2
United States of America	1	0
Egypt	4	3
Finland	1	1
Greece	3	2
Turkey	5	5
United Kingdom	1	1
China	20	15
Japan	4	3
New Zealand	1	1

STUDENT NOTE

In this list, China has the most prevalence of TB. Could this be because of the very widespread nature of the Chinese population, linked with the least health provision among wealthy nations?

It is interesting that Japan has significant TB among its population in spite of its high expenditure on health and longevity of its population.

Table 2.8 – **prevalence of current tobacco use among adults (≥15 years) (%), both sexes**

location	2005
Mexico	24.7
United States of America	23.9
Egypt	15.1
Finland	28.1
Greece	51.8
Turkey	35.5
United Kingdom	35.7
China	31.8
Japan	29.4
New Zealand	28.6

STUDENT NOTE

In this list, note that the UK still had significant tobacco use in 2005, although more recent statistics show that this figure may have fallen below 30%. It is possible that the single biggest cost to health systems is illness due to smoking tobacco.

Note that Greece has the highest tobacco use among this group, and Egypt the least. Why would this be the case?

Table 2.9 – **mortality rates for cancer and cardio-vascular diseases**

location	age-standardised mortality rate for cancer (per 100 000 population) 2002	age-standardised mortality rate for cardio-vascular diseases (per 100 000 population) 2002
Mexico	88	163
USA	134	188
Egypt	84	560
Finland	115	201
Greece	132	258
Turkey	95	542
UK	143	182
China	148	291
Japan	119	106
New Zealand	139	175

STUDENT NOTE

In this list, it might be possible to place links between tobacco use (table 2.8) and deaths due to cancer and cardio-vascular disease. Such links are very hard to prove. Note that the UK has a 20% higher incidence of cancer and a 72% higher incidence of cardio-vascular diseases than Japan. It is speculated that differences in diet could be the cause of these differences.

However, Egypt has the highest incidence of CVD, among the group, but the lowest proportion of people smoking, perhaps this negates the smoking link hypothesis?

Table 2.10 – **prevalence of adults, age ≥15 years, who are obese (from years 2000 to 2004 depending on country)**

location	(%) female	(%) male
Mexico	28.1	18.6
United States of America	33.2	31.1
Egypt	46.6	
Finland	13.5	14.9
Greece	18.2	26
Turkey	22.7	
United Kingdom	23	22.3
China	3.4	2.4
Japan	3.3	2.9
New Zealand	23.2	21.9

STUDENT NOTE

In this list Egypt's females are worst off, perhaps linked to ethnic issues?

However, the USA has a 10% higher incidence of obesity than the UK. Energy balance, lifestyle, and dietary issues are suggested as the reasons for this.

source: www.who.int/whosis/data/Search.jsp

Statistics

Students should research from **World Health Organisation** (WHO) websites to find the data that tells you what is happening in various countries of the world.

Data can include:
- Obesity.
- Mental health.
- Physical activity.
- Alcohol.
- Tobacco usage.
- Dental health.
- Diabetes.
- Cardio-vascular disease.
- Cancer.
- Bone disease.

Why is the population of Japan so healthy? It would not appear to be because the Japanese spend more on health, or because they smoke less. These statistics do not tell us about dietary habits – which could lead the Japanese to be less obese than anyone except the Chinese. They also do not tell us about attitudes to stress or family life. Physical stature might be a factor also – but these statistics do not include a measure of this factor. Students therefore should be careful when drawing conclusions from comparative statistics of this nature. Cause and effect are not always simple to spot. It seems to be a fact that Japanese people have a low but not the lowest rate of cancer among the groups looked at, and that the incidence of tuberculosis is higher than most western countries. So is it true that Japanese people are more healthy than we are?

Balanced lifestyle

Energy balance has been discussed at length above (pages 15 and 26), and its relationship to obesity or good health. This notion can be summed up as follows:

Positive energy balance (energy input via food > energy output via exercise) will lead eventually to obesity and high risk of CHD, diabetes and ill-health.

Neutral energy balance (energy input via food = energy output via exercise) will bring about a stable body mass and no worries about obesity.

Negative energy balance (energy input via food < energy output via exercise) will result in loss of body mass as adipose tissue is consumed to replace the energy shortfall.

Work-life balance

It is important to have a balance between the demands of work, exercise, social life and sleep. A lifestyle dominated by work and issues connected with work can lead to many of the sedentary lifestyle issues mentioned above.

Dealing with stress

As mentioned above (page 20), **stress** is a response of the body to any demands made on it and whose symptoms can be **physiological**, **psychological** or **behavioural**.

Stress can be dealt with in the following ways:
- Rest in a quiet place, try and sleep if possible.
- Reduce breathing rate, mental activity and muscle tension.
- Identify the stressors, take action, manage time effectively, and think positively.
- Keeping the body physically fit and in good health can help the individual manage stress and work towards living a healthy lifestyle.

Effects of ageing

The consequences of the ageing process (figure 2.8) are based on the maturing of a person's body structure. Unfortunately, maturation tends to equal deterioration unless an extensive exercise regime is undertaken – see above, page 19. The capability of the older person tends to reduce as he or she gets older, and the following discussion explains what is actually happening as age proceeds.

The term **ageing** includes all the changes that occur in the body as time progresses. **Arteriosclerosis, osteoporosis, osteoarthritis** (with reduced joint mobility), increased **body fat** and reduced **muscle mass** tend to reduce the capability of older people to undertake activities which younger people take for granted. The additional factors of economic deterioration and possible disability tend to reduce access to sporting provision.

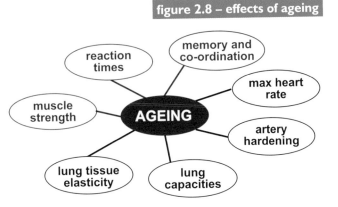

figure 2.8 – effects of ageing

Anaerobic decline with age

The following anaerobic effects are found as a person gets older:

- **Muscle** tends to reduce in size and function (**atrophy**) and therefore strength deteriorates with age.
- Maximal anaerobic power for both males and females **decreases** after 25 years of age. This is because there is a shift **towards slow twitch fibres**.
- Also, a thinner myelinated sheath to motor unit neurones **lengthens reaction times** which means that speed (and hence power) of muscle contraction is affected.
- A loss of neurones affects **short-term memory** and co-ordination.

There is evidence that older people who continue **anaerobic** (power) exercises maintain **strength** up to the level of an untrained person of 20 years of age. Figure 2.9 shows how strength decreases with age.

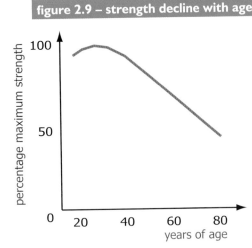

figure 2.9 – strength decline with age

Aerobic decline with age

This decline (figure 2.10) is in terms of low intensity activity:

- For the **cardio-vascular** system, there is a decline in maximum heart rate (**HR**$_{max}$ = 220 – age) and stroke volume, and hence cardiac output.
- There is an increase in **resting pulse rate** due to decreased cardiac stroke volume (SV).
- **Artery hardening** (arteriosclerosis) increases resting systolic blood pressure.
- Heart rate **recovery** takes longer after exercise.

- For the **respiratory** system, maximal oxygen uptake ($\dot{V}O_{2max}$) declines at about 10% per decade due to reduction in SV (cardiac stroke volume) and maximum heart rate. This would be caused by lack of aerobic exercise.
- The lung vital capacity (**VC**) and **forced expiratory volume** decrease with age. Further, the lung residual volume (**RV**) becomes larger hence there would be less air exchanged per breath.
- The **elasticity of alveoli walls** and reduced strength of respiratory muscles also decreases $\dot{V}O_{2max}$.
- Arterio-venous oxygen difference (**a-$\bar{v}O_{2diff}$**) reduces since less oxygen is extracted by muscles.

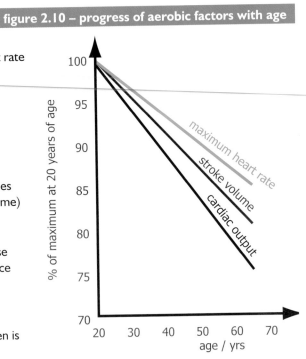

figure 2.10 – progress of aerobic factors with age

Most **fitness measures fall** after the age of about 25. Note that **trained** individuals' fitness levels start at a higher point and do not fall as far as those of **untrained** individuals.

Effects of exercise

As mentioned above, the effects of exercise are:

- To slow down and reduce the effects of degenerative diseases like **CHD**.
- To increase **high density lipoproteins** (HDL-C) and decrease **low density lipoproteins** (LDL-C are responsible for depositing cholesterol and narrowing lumina of arteries), hence blood pressure tends to be stable thus **preventing hypertension**.
- To slow down the decline in $\dot{V}O_{2max}$.
- To reduce **obesity** by burning off excess fat during and after activity when metabolic rate remains elevated. This helps the functioning of the heart since **cardiac workload** is less with lower body mass.
- To relieve symptoms of **osteoarthritis** and reduce **osteoporosis**.
- To sustain **strength** and **co-ordination** levels and enhance **tensile strength** and **flexibility** of tendons and ligaments thus allowing for a fuller range of **joint movement**.

Body composition

The following table 2.11 show how the body fat content for people of various age groups depends on whether they are fit or not. The data takes us up to 40 years of age.

Table 2.11 – **example data of relative body fat values for untrained and trained males and females**

| age group | relative body fat (%) | | | |
| | untrained | | trained | |
	females	males	females	males
15-19	20-24	13-16	12-20	7-13
20-29	22-25	15-20	10-18	6-12
30-39	24-30	18-26	12-20	8-14

STUDENT NOTE

The **average body fat** for **untrained females** is about 8% higher than untrained males. However, **trained females** are exceptionally lean and their relative body fat values are **well below** those values for untrained males. Therefore **females** can **reduce fat stores** well below what is considered normal for their age.

Untrained males and females have increased body fat when they get older, whereas trained people (both sexes) remain lean.

Factors affecting flexibility

As people get older:

- Bony **features** of a **joint** change due to arthritic conditions within joints.
- The length and position of **tendons and ligaments** change as strength is lost leading to joint instability and dislocations.
- **Elasticity of muscle tissue** changes as muscle function declines leading to postural difficulties such as kyphosis.
- The **elasticity of skin** changes to increase flabbiness.

All these factors change to **decrease flexibility** with age.

Metabolic rate changes with age

Total metabolic rate (**TMR**) is a combination of energy expenditure of the body due to all processes (see page 23 above):

- The **BMR** (basal metabolic rate) = rate of energy expenditure while at rest.
- The **SDA** (specific dynamic action) = extra rate of energy expenditure due to digestion, absorption of nutrients, and transport of nutrients to body cells, usually estimated as **10% of energy value of food** consumed.
- Energy expenditure due to exercise.

TMR = all energy expenditure due to exercise + BMR + SDA

TMR is usually worked out for each kilogram of body mass, for each minute.

Table 2.12 – **average rates of energy expenditure (total metabolic rate) for men and women living in the USA**

age	men		women	
	kJ per day	kJ kg⁻¹ min⁻¹	kJ per day	kJ kg⁻¹ min⁻¹
15 - 18	12,500	0.132	9,200	0.116
19 - 24	12,100	0.117	9,200	0.11
25 - 50	12,100	0.107	9,200	0.101
50+	9,640	0.087	7,900	0.085

STUDENT NOTE

The figures for kJ kg⁻¹ min⁻¹ are corrected for the average body mass of the group.

Source: Essentials of Exercise Physiology 3e, McArdle, Katch and Katch, Lippincott, Williams & Wilkins 2006.

The importance of this data is that people over 50 use and require 10% to 20% less energy for their daily activity. Hence it would be necessary to eat 10% to 20% less food to maintain a neutral energy balance and keep a constant body mass.

Practice questions

1) What are the purposes of the three main groups of food? *3 marks*

2) How can an athlete's diet aid the recovery process? *2 marks*

3) You have been asked to provide some nutritional strategies for an elite swimmer competing in seven races in the Regional Championships in a week's time. What can you recommend? *3 marks*

4) Provide recommendations for carbohydrate, fat and protein intake for a cross-country skier and a ski jumper. Give reasons for your recommendations. *6 marks*

5) Outline **five** different physiological effects of ageing on the human body. *5 marks*

6) Explain how exercise can reduce the effects of ageing. *8 marks*

7) Osteoporosis refers to a loss of bone mass that occurs with ageing.
Identify **two** major contributing factors common to post-menopausal females.
What is the most desirable form of exercise that would slow down the rate of skeletal ageing and why? *4 marks*

8) Discuss the value of consuming carbohydrates during and after endurance-based exercise. *4 marks*

9) a) Define what is meant by the term obesity and give percentage values that are considered to represent obese norms for both males and females. *3 marks*
b) Table 2.13 shows the current trends in obesity levels for 15 year olds and above in comparative global cultures.
Using the data in table 2.13 suggest reasons why percentage levels vary so much between countries. *6 marks*

Table 2.13 – **prevalence of adults, age ≥15 years, who are obese**

location	(%) female	(%) male
Mexico	28.1	18.6
United States of America	33.2	31.1
Egypt	46.6	
Finland	13.5	14.9
United Kingdom	23	22.3
China	3.4	2.4
Japan	3.3	2.9
New Zealand	23.2	21.9

CHAPTER 3: *Effects of exercise – responses and adaptations of the body systems – the muscular system*

Musculo-skeletal system

STUDENT NOTE A general overview of the structure of the musculo-skeletal system is required, but will not be directly examined, so we include a general overview here.

Introduction

The skeletal system

The **functions** of the skeletal system are to act as a lever system, as surface area for attachment of muscle, tendons and ligaments, and to give shape and support to the body. Also, red / white blood cells are manufactured within bone marrow, and bones store fats and minerals.

Types of skeletal connective tissue

There are two types of skeletal connective tissue, cartilage and bone.

Cartilage

Cartilage is a firm, smooth, resilient, non-vascular connective tissue. There are three types of cartilage found in the human body:

- **Hyaline (articular) cartilage** has a smooth, solid matrix which sits on the ends of bones, and forms the exact surfaces which are in contact and move across one another when a joint is used.
- **White fibro-cartilage** is tough and slightly flexible and exists between vertebrae.
- **Yellow elastic cartilage** is soft and elastic and exists in the ear lobes.

Hyaline cartilage works by absorbing synovial fluid from the joint spaces when it is not under pressure, and then expelling this fluid when it comes into contact with another cartilagenous surface. This means that when high impact exercise is taken, and a joint has forces exerted through it, the articular surfaces at each side of the joint (the hyaline cartilage on the ends of the bones at opposite sides of the joint) in effect mould themselves one into the other as this fluid is expelled. This is a moveable situation (as the joint surfaces move) and relies on the cartilage being able to absorb this fluid when the pressure is off.

Added features of this situation are that the expelled fluid reduces friction between the moving surfaces, and that the slightly spongy cartilage tissue provides a cushion to reduce impact forces when the long bones in a joint come together forcefully.

This theory of how a cartilage works is called **McCutchen**'s weeping theory of lubrication.

The structure and function of bone tissue

Bone is classified as either hard (or compact), or spongy (or cancellous). It is the hardest connective tissue in the human body, and is composed of water, organic material (mainly collagen), and inorganic salts, namely calcium phosphate, calcium carbonate, and fluoride salts.

- The **periosteum** is an outer protective covering of bone which provides attachment for muscle tendons and ligaments. The deeper layers of the periosteum are responsible for growth in bone **width**.
- The **epiphyseal disc** or growth plate is the segment of a bone in which an increase in bone **length** takes place.
- **Compact bone** (shown in figure 3.1) consists of dense, tightly packed, ring shaped calcium phosphate plates. This forms solid bone tissue and is located down the shaft of a long bone and the outer layers of short, flat and irregular bones. Its dense structure gives strength and support.

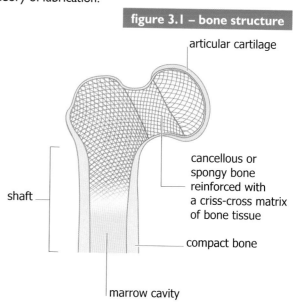

figure 3.1 – bone structure

articular cartilage

shaft

cancellous or spongy bone reinforced with a criss-cross matrix of bone tissue

compact bone

marrow cavity

- **Cancellous bone** has a lattice-like (honeycomb) spongy appearance reinforced by a criss-cross matrix of bone tissue. It is light-weight and is located at the ends of a long bone (figure 3.1), in addition to providing the internal bone tissue in short, flat and irregular bones.

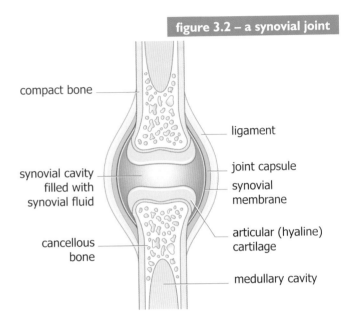

figure 3.2 – a synovial joint

compact bone

ligament

joint capsule

synovial cavity filled with synovial fluid

synovial membrane

cancellous bone

articular (hyaline) cartilage

medullary cavity

The articular system

Joints

Articulation is defined 'as a place where two or more bones meet to form a joint'.

Joint types are:

- **Fibrous or immovable** – for example, between bones of the cranium.
- **Cartilaginous or slightly moveable** – for example, vertebral discs.
- **Synovial or freely moveable**.

Synovial joint

- See figure 3.2 for the locations of the elements of a synovial joint.
- **Synovial fluid** reduces joint friction by lubrication, and maintains joint stability.
- **Synovial membrane** encloses fluid and secretes fluid.
- **Joint capsule** is a sleeve of tough, fibrous tissue surrounding the joint.
- **Ligament** is an extension of the joint capsule consisting of strong, fibrous connective tissue that provides stability by joining bone to bone.
- **Articular cartilage** prevents friction between bones, and cushions the ends of bones.
- **Bursae** prevent friction and wear.
- **Pads of fat** cushion the joint.
- **Menisci** (formed from hyaline cartilage) help bones fit together and improve stabilisation of the joint.

Short-term responses of the skeletal system to exercise

The lever systems provided by bones at joints, enable the skeletal system to exert forces on its surroundings. Both bone and cartilage is slightly elastic when subjected to force, which means that they won't shatter or break when exercised (usually!).

Mostly the skeletal system reacts inertly to exercise, excepting the cartilagenous structures which absorb and release synovial fluid from joints when forces are exerted (according to McCutchen's weeping theory of lubrication).

Long-term responses of the skeletal system to exercise

As mentioned in Chapter 2 page 24 above, osteoporosis is an age-related condition of bone which can evolve when a person is inactive. Osteoporosis occurs largely because bone is not stimulated by stress (mechanical stress produced by weight bearing activities). Bone tends to respond to force by becoming stronger – as do most biological systems. The cell structure can change with cell walls becoming thicker and therefore stronger.

The opposite of this is the fact that if bone is **not stressed**, its cells become thinner walled and hence weaker. Extreme evidence for this was given by bone analysis on Russian astronauts on return from six months in the space station. The astronauts had lost up to 60% of bone mass compared to before taking off. They were able to recover bone mass within 12 months by hard exercise. Astronauts now have a compulsory exercise programme to try and reduce this effect.

Cyclists and swimmers (whose exercise produces relatively less mechanical bone stress) have more of a tendency to osteoporosis in later life than joggers or aerobics participants.

Other adaptations of the skeletal system produced by exercise are:

- Thickening of articular cartilage provides greater cushioning and protection of bone ends from wear and tear.
- Improvement of the capability of the hyaline cartilage to absorb and release synovial fluid (according to McCutchen's theory) when pressure is reduced and increased.
- Increased range of movement at a joint.
- These adaptations enable an athlete to progress to higher intensity impact work within training programmes such as in plyometrics, weight lifting and gymnastics.

Muscles of the human body

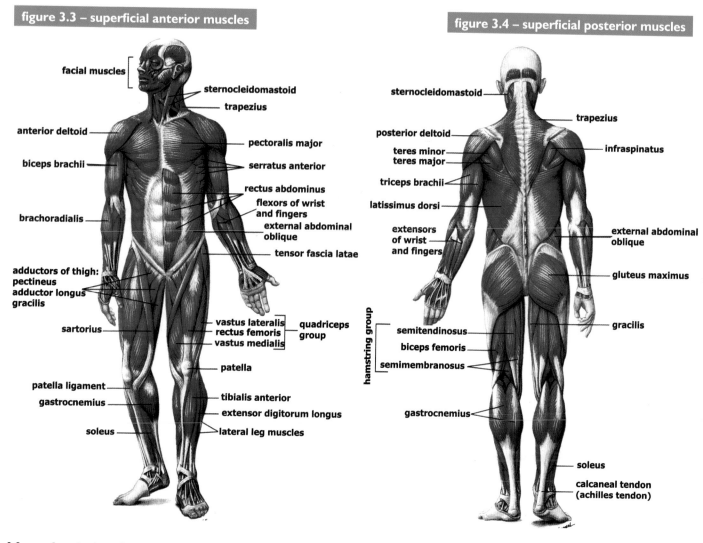

figure 3.3 – superficial anterior muscles

facial muscles
sternocleidomastoid
trapezius
anterior deltoid
pectoralis major
biceps brachii
serratus anterior
rectus abdominus
flexors of wrist and fingers
brachoradialis
external abdominal oblique
tensor fascia latae
adductors of thigh:
pectineus
adductor longus
gracilis
sartorius
vastus lateralis
rectus femoris
vastus medialis
quadriceps group
patella
patella ligament
gastrocnemius
tibialis anterior
extensor digitorum longus
soleus
lateral leg muscles

figure 3.4 – superficial posterior muscles

sternocleidomastoid
trapezius
posterior deltoid
teres minor
teres major
infraspinatus
triceps brachii
latissimus dorsi
extensors of wrist and fingers
external abdominal oblique
gluteus maximus
gracilis
hamstring group
semitendinosus
biceps femoris
semimembranosus
gastrocnemius
soleus
calcaneal tendon (achilles tendon)

Musculo-skeletal attachments

Ligaments attach bone to bone to limit the range of movement of joints.
Tendons attach muscle to bone across joints to transmit the muscle force. They are strong and mainly inelastic – for example the Achilles tendon attaches the gastrocnemius muscle to the periosteal bone tissue of calcaneus or the heel bone.

Origins and insertion of muscles

The tendon at the static end of the muscle is called the **origin** and the tendon at the end of the muscle closest to the joint that moves is called the **insertion** of that muscle.

Antagonistic muscle action

This term describes the fact that muscles work in pairs (see figure 3.5).

- The **agonist** is the active muscle, the muscle under tension or doing work and functioning as the **prime mover** of a joint during the desired movement.
- The **antagonist** relaxes to allow the agonist to work as movement occurs.
- For example, curling a bar, the agonist = **biceps brachii muscle**, and the antagonist = **triceps brachii muscle.**

figure 3.5 – muscle function – curling a bar

agonist (biceps) · antagonist (triceps) · synergist (trapezius) · fixator (deltoid)

A **synergist muscle** holds the body in position so that an agonist muscle can operate, thus preventing any unwanted movements that might occur as the prime mover contracts. For example, the trapezius muscle holds the shoulder in place during the bar curling exercise.

A **fixator** muscle by definition is a synergist muscle, but is more specifically referred to as a **fixator** or **stabiliser** when it immobilises the bone of the prime mover's origin, thus providing a stable base for the action of the prime mover. For example, the deltoid muscle stabilises the scapula during a bar curl.

Muscle fibre structure

There are three types of muscle tissue in the human body.

- **Involuntary** / smooth / visceral muscle, which is found within the walls of blood vessels – the tunica media (see page 55 below) and the alimentary canal.
- **Cardiac** muscle, which forms the walls of the heart – the myocardium (see page 48 below).
- **Skeletal** muscle, which is the muscle type concerned with human movement and activity.

Skeletal muscle tissue

Skeletal muscle (also called striated voluntary muscle in that microscopic bands or striations can be seen) attaches to bone and is responsible for the following functions:

- **Producing** movement by exerting force on its origin and insertion.
- **Maintaining** body posture and changing body shape.
- **Generating** heat to keep us warm.
- **Storage** of glycogen for energy.

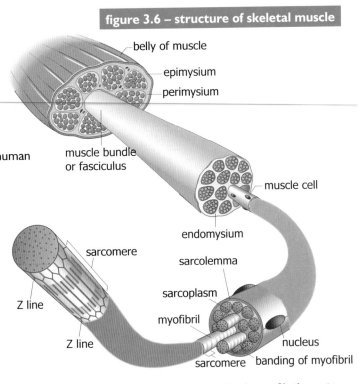

figure 3.6 – structure of skeletal muscle

belly of muscle · epimysium · perimysium · muscle bundle or fasciculus · muscle cell · endomysium · sarcolemma · sarcoplasm · myofibril · nucleus · banding of myofibril · sarcomere · Z line · Z line · sarcomere

Figure 3.6 shows the basic structure of a muscle from the muscle belly down to the individual sarcomere. Each myofibril consists of filaments of actin (thin filaments) and myosin (thick filaments) the forces between which enable a muscle to shorten its length and hence contract and exert forces on its origin and insertion.

An action potential

Transmission of neural messages along a neurone is an electrochemical process. An **action potential** is initiated when sufficient numbers of sodium ions (Na^+) diffuse into the neurone. This depolarises the axon to a critical threshold level called the **all-or-none law**. This is followed by repolarisation back to the resting potential. This process forms an electrical impulse which then transmits itself down the neurone (see figure 3.14). In effect this electrical impulse is **conducted** down the axon. The **myelin sheath** insulates the axon, and the action potential travels from node to node in a wave like action, since ion exchange only occurs at the nodes of Ranvier.

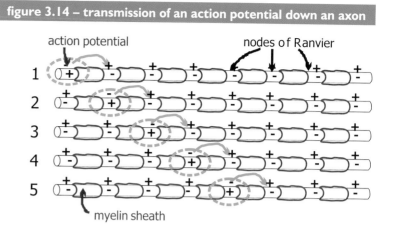

figure 3.14 – transmission of an action potential down an axon

The nerve action potential is followed by the muscle action potential. A delay of 0.5 milliseconds occurs due to release of transmitter substances (such as acetylcholine from synaptic knobs) which initiate the muscle action potential. The area of depolarisation travels down a muscle cell passing the entrances to 'T' vesicles which secrete calcium ions needed to initiate muscle contraction.

Each different muscle fibre type (slow twitch or fast twitch) is innervated by a separate and different type of motor neurone.

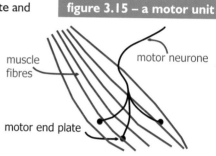

figure 3.15 – a motor unit

The motor end plate

The function of the motor end plate is to transfer an impulse from the motor neurones (see figure 3.15) to the muscle fibre block. This causes all muscle fibres attached to this end plate to contract.

Synapse

- A synapse is a junction where the axon of one neurone interacts with another neurone. Figure 3.16 outlines the process whereby the nerve impulse is transmitted from the neurone via the synapse to the muscle bed.

- This process involves the use of calcium ions (Ca^{++}) to trigger the release of a substance called acetylcholine (Ach) which then jumps into receptor sites in the motor end plate attached to the muscle fibre.

- This in turn triggers release of sodium ions (Na^+) which re-establish the action potential within the muscle fibre itself (and eventually cause it to contract and use energy).

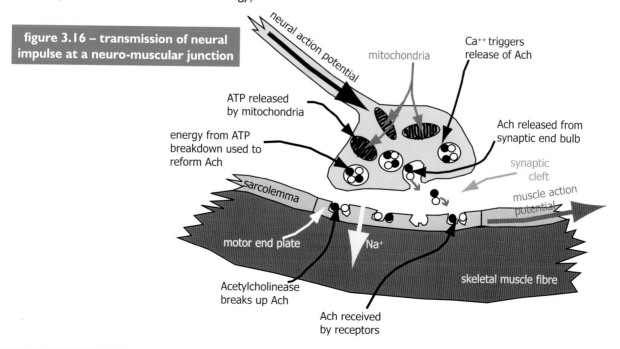

figure 3.16 – transmission of neural impulse at a neuro-muscular junction

Motor neural firing patterns

In order to control muscle contraction, the cerebellum innervates one or more motor units. Each motor unit controls a number of fibres, so that either **all** the fibres attached to the motor unit are activated at the same time, or **none** of these fibres are activated. This is called the '**all-or-none law**'. Different fibre groups (attached to different motor units) are fired at different times. Each firing produces a fibre '**twitch**'.

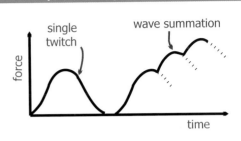

figure 3.17 – force produced by a single fibre twitch

The force produced by a single fibre twitch follows the left hand graph in figure 3.17. Note that each twitch only lasts a short length of time, so that in order to prolong the force exerted by a twitch, the fibre group must be fired repeatedly. The build up of force in a single fibre is represented in the right hand graph in figure 3.17. When a fibre is fired repeatedly in this manner, the way in which the force builds up is called '**wave summation**'.

Multiple fibre twitches

In order to activate fibres across a whole muscle body to produce force in a controlled manner, different fibre groups are fired in succession. The total force across the space of a muscle is the sum of the effect of different fibre groups, and is shown in figure 3.18. This is called '**spatial summation**'.

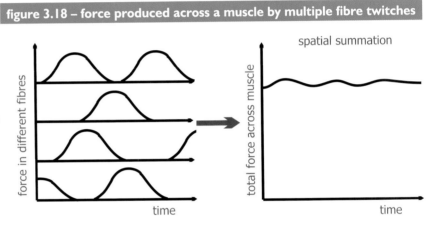

figure 3.18 – force produced across a muscle by multiple fibre twitches

In order to control very fine movements, it is necessary to be able to vary the total force produced by fibre twitches. **Gradation of contraction** refers to the ability of muscle to produce forces varying from very light to maximum force or tension.

This can be achieved in two ways:

- Increasing the frequency of stimulus (wave summation).
- Varying the number of motor units recruited.

For example in hockey, there would be fine control of movement required for a flick, as opposed to the maximum effort required for a full hit.

If there were no time for relaxation between motor unit firing, eventually (after a few seconds) there would be a complete lock up of muscle. This is called '**tetanine contraction**' and happens when a muscle is used at maximum for too long.

The cerebellum

The balance of fine and gross control is under the control of the **cerebellum**. In order to produce smooth co-ordinated movement, the cerebellum compares the intended movement with the actual movement (from sensors within the moving structure – the proprioceptors). If a difference is detected, the cerebellum sends impulses to the appropriate motor units in the spinal cord which would produce a correction. In sport, the cerebellum is involved in the learning of **fine motor skills** (as in archery) or **gross motor skills** (as in weight lifting).

Gross movements use leg and arm muscles having about 1000 muscle fibres associated with one motor unit, whereas fine movements (of the eyes and fingers for example) require muscles with far fewer (10-100) muscle fibres controlled by a single motor unit.

Control is achieved by increasing or decreasing the number of motor units in operation. Different motor units are activated in turn across a muscle and this gradation of contraction across a muscle enables very small forces to be maintained if required. The self-regulation of rhythmic movements between one muscle and its antagonist relies on control of movement which requires relaxation of antagonists during the dynamic activity of an agonist. This process is called '**reciprocal innervation**'.

Adaptations to muscle cells produced by exercise – the long-term responses

Table 3.2 displays the adaptations to skeletal muscle cells produced by different types of exercise.

Table 3.2 – **adaptations produced by exercise**

adaptations to muscle cells produced by anaerobic exercise	adaptations to muscle cells produced by aerobic training
fast twitch muscle **hypertrophy** - increase in size by increased cross sectional area of a muscle	**body fat** proportion is reduced by between 4% and 12%
increase in the number of **myofibrils** within each muscle cell	more **myoglobin** is created in muscle cells
increase in the **sarcoplasmic** volume within each cell	more and bigger **mitochondria** are created in muscle cells
increase in the size and strength of the contractile proteins, **actin and myosin**, leading to increase in the mass of fast twitch fibres	muscle cells have increased **oxidative enzymes** which increases aerobic cell activity
increase in the number of fast twitch muscle fibres (**hyperplasia**), which means that the proportion of type II muscle fibre increases and the proportion of type I decreases	increase in utilisation of **fat** in adipose tissue as an energy source
increase in muscle **cell stores** of substances such as ATP, PC, and glycogen, and increase in anaerobic enzymes such as creatine kinase (CK), PFK, GPP, and LDH, which makes the muscle stronger and more powerful	increase in stores of **glycogen** in muscle which enables more fuel to be available for aerobic work
improved toleration of **lactate** in fast twitch fibres, and improved ability to remove lactate from muscle cell into blood - which enhances lactate thresholds and **reduces OBLA**	**conversion** of type IIb to type IIa fibres, so increasing the proportion of aerobically active muscle cells
increased rate of response of **CNS** (Central Nervous System), **recruitment** of additional **fast twitch** fibre motor units, improved co-ordination of fast twitch fibre motor units	better **recruitment** of **slow twitch** fibre motor units making muscle usage more efficient
toughening of **proprioceptors** so that more force is required to stimulate inhibitory signals, an improved agonist antagonist response	
reduction of **delayed onset muscle soreness** (**DOMS**)	reduction of **delayed onset muscle soreness** (**DOMS**)

figure 3.19 – muscle hypertrophy in a body builder

STUDENT NOTE

The increase in muscle mass caused by hypertrophy (see figure 3.19) will increase the proportion of muscle to body fat and help reduce obesity. Increased storage of ATP and phosphocreatine (PC) will increase the strength or efficiency of each fast twitch muscle fibre.

Improved lactate handling enhances alactic / lactate and lactate / aerobic thresholds, and causes a delay in the onset of blood lactate accumulation (**OBLA**). These processes enable an improved capacity of alactic (ATP-PC) and lactic acid systems to resynthesise ATP, and hence to deliver energy more rapidly. Also there would be increases in maximum possible peak power, and the ability to maintain maximal power output for longer. There would be a decrease in delayed onset muscle soreness (**DOMS**), particularly following eccentric training.

The adaptations in which more muscle fibres are recruited within an activity will better utilise fast twitch muscle fibres at their existing level before hypertrophy occurs. Initial measured strength gains are almost exclusively via this process.

figure 3.20 – a female bodybuilder with muscle hypertrophy

STUDENT NOTE

The adaptive response depends on an individual's fitness, cultural norms, gender, psychological preparedness and state of maturation. Given that anaerobic training will have the above effects, the outcomes will vary between individuals. Particularly, female athletes will acquire muscle hypertrophy if exposed to high intensity anaerobic exercise (figure 3.20).

Practice questions

1) Critically evaluate the positive impacts of participating in different types of physical activity on the joints and muscles of the human body.
12 marks

2) Skeletal muscle contains both slow and fast twitch muscle fibres but the proportion of each depends upon the function of a muscle as a whole. Table 3.3 lists some of the differences between slow and fast twitch muscle fibres.

Table 3.3 – **muscle fibre type characteristics**

characteristic	slow twitch type	fast twitch type
contractile time / ms	110	40
mitochondrial density	high	low
glycogen store	low	high
phosphocreatine stores	low	high
capillary density	high	low
sarcoplasmic reticulum	poorly developed	well developed
oxidative enzyme activity	high	low

a) Suggest why the muscles concerned in maintaining the trunk posture of the body of the sprinter might be expected to have a larger percentage of slow twitch muscle fibres.
Using table 3.3 explain why fast twitch muscle fibres may build up an oxygen debt during a 400m sprint.   *5 marks*
b) Account for the difference in the speed of contraction between slow and fast twitch muscle fibre types.
Fast twitch muscle fibres are divided into two types, IIa and IIb. Identify the major functional characteristic between these sub groups.
In what sporting activities would the adaptation of fast twitch type IIb to type IIa fibres be relevant to a sportsperson?
6 marks

3) Briefly describe the structure of a skeletal muscle fibre, and explain how it contracts when stimulated.   *5 marks*